T*Æ* H*OW*
IN THE *W*ORLD

by

Louise Longson

First published 2025 by The Hedgehog Poetry Press,

5 Coppack House, Churchill Avenue, Clevedon. BS21 6QW

www.hedgehogpress.co.uk

ISBN: 978-1-916830-57-8

Cover image © Oormila Vijayakrishnan Prahlad

To Mark – the who, why and what in my world

Contents

"The world is the mirror of myself dying." 7

How we are the willows that weep by the banks of the river 8

Memories Left by Water 9

The Impact of Atmospheric Change on Bird Flight 10

Hunger Stones 12

Transhumance: The Movement of Sheep 13

Dark Harvest (26 March 2022) 14

Liquid that flowed in the veins of the god of war 15

Spirit Bear 16

How We Are The Movement of Water in Trees 18

Somewhere in the Shadows 19

how we are like the moon 22

3D Printed Rechargeable Planet Night Light 23

Prayer for the Bodies of Those Who Died Violently 24

In the half-light on the day war breaks out 26

Finding A Piece of Humanity 27

Do not stand too close 28

Sonnet for the Sailors of the Eduard Bohlen 29

How We Are Something Sharp Smoothed by Sea 30

Depth of Field 31

Graveyard by the Sea 32

"THE WORLD IS THE MIRROR OF MYSELF DYING."

(Henry Miller)

Like a toad
eating its own skin,
I can taste nothingness,
the scoured-shell emptiness
of what will come—

a ghostly glamour reflected
in an open void—

a world under water
where only an echo
of our flowering
will haunt infinity
scenting its shadows
like fading breath.

HOW WE ARE THE WILLOWS THAT WEEP BY THE BANKS OF THE RIVER

ochrebrown ophidian riverrise
serpentines across flooded fields
her swollen belly sick with forever

substances/slurry/silage/silt/sewage
stinking with degradation
that will take a thousand years

fragmented

by weir/dam/culver/ford/sluice

here in the oncerich water
glass elvers wound sinuous
silver-threading their way
upstream from the sea

over-abstraction has left us
with empty reality
filled only by the greenslick
of algae and acid

water

the deadzone
where caddisflies build
coffincases from the debris

MEMORIES LEFT BY WATER

(the River Severn, Bronze Age – Anthropocene)

by the once-sacred river   under the disused footbridge

broken swords   sharps and condoms

votive offerings   among the effluvia

a remembrance   the spilling

of royal blood   of spent passion

THE IMPACT OF ATMOSPHERIC CHANGE ON BIRD FLIGH

I have flown

too long   exhausted
stranded

    drowning
       in creeping sands

feathers splayed   pulled
by forever

     rougher tides

that strip
and
slough   my skin

see what held me

together

what clutched tight

    how   *nerves* *locked*
stiffened
sinews   *pumped*   *muscles*
   pinions
  readied for flight

until at last   I tear   apart
from
        all the ties
                to my home-
        land
                open skies

are hostile   now

my bones   are   breaking
            with my heart

HUNGER STONES

""We cried, we cry, and you will cry."
(Carving on a stone revealed during the 2023 drought, river Elbe, Tuchlovice, Czech
Republic)

Low water surfaces
scar-carved
initials of authors lost
to our history.

Now, the earth is hot and charred.

Crops are hurting, soil starves,
rivers are dust-
dry, skeletons
of broken
        architecture
flaunt bones
chiselled with hardship,

scrimshawed
with pain,

turned to rust
like bombs and grenades
sunk in this veteran silt,

now awakened, again.

Again.

TRANSHUMANCE: THE MOVEMENT OF SHEEP

Wily circling dogs
bite at their heels, barking
with borrowed authority,

urging them on to another patch
of gated land: fenced-in
low territory, a holding-pen.

They swirl and stir
steaming in the shank
of daybreak,

voices raised
in urgent calls
to their kin;

a refugee flock
driven forward by hunger,

pent-up strength,
and half-forgotten memories
of higher, sweeter pastures

where winter violets'
purple hearts pierced
the soaked earth, clustered
like grumes, deep-
drenched, deep-
rooted, clenched in the humus
of decay.

DARK HARVEST (26 MARCH 2022)

for Gruinard Island, former MoD biological warfare testing ground

This is not the first time
the island has been baptized
by fire.

Seeds, spores, germs
lay deep in the black soil's
memory of that tiny moment:

of white powder clouds pluming
on the wind, releasing death;

of blown-out carcasses incinerated
or buried under the rubble

of blown-up cliffs by the shores;

of leaving the island alone

to breed and brood, preserved in spite

of formaldehyde washes and sprays
of seawater.

Smoke drifts across the channel
as the heather burns. Scorched
skies cover an appalled dawn
with a shroud made of ghosts.

All that is left now are stripped remains
of trees standing sentry on the shoreline—
naked skeletons broken in waves
of flame; the screaming of birds;

the silence.

LIQUID THAT FLOWED IN THE VEINS OF THE GOD OF WAR

sudden summer rain
                    falls

like liquid that flowed

in the veins of the god   of war

metallic   scent
        rises
                susurrating
memories

of burned earth
                and
                        wasted

        blood

SPIRIT BEAR

Pale ghost stares
through the water
sees
the salmon writhe

muscle-lithe
in river-shallows

she is unseen
against the bright sky.

Today she hunts
in the deep hollows
where magic
hides.

Her haunts
are darkful of shadows
beneath the cedars
where bones
of dead fish
fertilize the ground.

In the brown of dusk,
from their nest high
in the boughs, ravens
curfew-call.

As she bends to the river
white fur brushes
red
cedar beams

breaking

the single thread
of spider-silk
attached
to what is left
of her disappearing world.

HOW WE ARE THE MOVEMENT OF WATER IN TREES

the flick of a tongue-
quick isness; life
in the deadwood,
a thing in and of itself,

a noumenon, rising up
from where we are rooted
in a phloem-flow
phenomenon.

Tiny stomate hearts hammer
with the wonder of being

open and close

on the surface of leaves

where the soul of water transpires
in the surface tension
of fluid dynamics

        we leave
            unleave

                fall

SOMEWHERE IN THE SHADOWS

1.
solid ground always breaks
into a climb
only a short way into a cave

turnings become tighter,
steep rises pull
unused muscles,

aching dark
tears
at eyes and breath

becomes a keening
as the wet stone cries
sharp stalactites

2.
Listen:
Orestes' bones
intone eternal songs

from the dead-wood kindling
at the bottom of the barque

from the jawbone
of a makeshift harp
strings are struck
by a war-wasted hero's hand

Look:
his spine-cracked skeleton is sculled
home to a greener land

3.
In another life, I am this
blackbird, perching
on a rusting climbing frame

rummaging in undergrowth
for chthonic creatures,
chattering in the rustle of beeches,

scattering burnt umber and bone-
brown leaves;
skittering
under ashes, in a breadth of shade,
pitched and blown
by a wind that screeches.

4.
in the 1970s and1980s
the packages started arriving
with fired bullets
encased in the pigment

from the ever-green tree
sticky
with history dripping
toxic with time

clothed in soft-dyed robes
of gamboge

he breathed his life away.

Colours are sometimes soaked in blood.

5.
Somewhere in the shadows
a rose blooms unnoticed

petals crimson the dark

unseen flames burn
scarlet weals
of yearning
turning raw leaving scars

at the very heart
of us
all
these violet wounds
agape

HOW WE ARE LIKE THE MOON

shrinking

it is only natural
after a hot birth
the violence
of impact
as planets
coalesce
collide

getting
cooler
brittle

breaking

into fault-

lines that are
at first nothing
more than wrinkles
in time

but turn
into stair-steep
cliffs and

chasms
leaving scars   visible   in   the void

3D PRINTED RECHARGEABLE PLANET NIGHT LIGHT

and somewhere deep in a night of broken ice
and sleep I feel an assuasive moon caressing
the shivering sky reassuring it against losses
whispering and pretending that the old magic
still exists (*as it was in the beginning*) yet

this world of promise lies in fragments in the play
of a card the press of a button in its dying throes
the planet (*is now*) just a monumental body an effigy
a replica in plastic a death-mask facsimile in three
dimensions (*and ever shall be*) convincing to no-one

PRAYER FOR THE BODIES OF THOSE WHO DIED VIOLENT

(Sutton Hoo)

In this place, a blank bank of sand
holds our broken bodies
like a breath.

forgive us

Acid ground has preserved us
in our final agonies, with grace;

all our sins

beached between our lives'
transgressions

our trespasses

we are stranded in death
trying to find a path

lead us

from this earth we cannot leave
to a heaven

not into temptation

we may never reach

deliver us

And what can you learn from sand?

from evil

We all become echoes;
faint whispers on air, shadows
on this land, in the briefest brush
of sun.

Thy will be done

IN THE HALF-LIGHT ON THE DAY WAR BREAKS OUT

red kites circle together
against the lowering sun

turning
molten bronze

pouring copper-
red and rust.

A solitary black crow sails straight
as a bullet

home
to the oncoming dusk.

Swifts rake the skies,
untrammelled

cries drift

and meld in the stillness.

In the stream
a diaspora of silver minnows

scatters
into shadows
and dust.

FINDING A PIECE OF HUMANITY

Nests have come down
from the ivy that clings
to the empty house.

Woven among twigs,
feathers, fragile skeletons

of leaves like handmade lace,
wreathed threads of green
tamarisk moss:

a piece
of them—
a curl of hair
that someone cut short

in the garden
that last spring—

cinder-grey
as shadows,
bomb-dust
and ash.

DO NOT STAND TOO CLOSE

there are uncertain cliffs
by the shore
where storm-winds
flow along the bluffs.

There are boulders
that can tumble

rocks

that can crush.

Take care near mountains.

Cold air
hurls down valleys
and violent katabatic winds rush.

Until the storm-winds straighten
and disappear
like chasing smoke

do not stand too close
to the edges
or the end
of the Earth.

SONNET FOR THE SAILORS OF THE EDUARD BOHLEN

(Skeleton Coast, Namibia)

You do not have to sail to see
where the ship's bones are,
(a thousand feet from water)
resting on wind-whipped waves of dunes.

Time's relentless plane has sanded
it to a desert sea that sailors shadows haunt,
(a thousand feet from water)
that smooths their bones hour by hour,

blanched and bleached in the glower
of an absolute sun, where it never rains.
(a thousand feet from water)
They traded their lives for eternity.

See now: where jackals crouch beneath it
as time creeps in by grains.

HOW WE ARE SOMETHING SHARP SMOOTHED BY SEA

rough edges rubbed
into soft-

sanded

nacreous shell-scars

shimmering
striae   stretched

frayed sailcloth

sanded

a hagstone hole

where winds whistle
through

whittled whalebone
written on by time

scrimshawed
jetsam   stranded

lodged in the rock-
pools with kelp
and bladderwrack
for company

waiting for the ebb-
tide flow

into the deep
where the waves
know us

DEPTH OF FIELD

Miles inland, the sea is
a distant thought-horizon.

Yet they are here: a proclamation
of gulls picking among the corn-brash,

cries keening like knives
over sharp stones,

charming the worms
by stamping their feet

on the jagged bed—undersheeted
by the clag of clay,
the guano stink—

they pluck the smallest
mite from broken ground
where the reliquiae of once-living
creatures lie unmourned.

GRAVEYARD BY THE SEA

(after Paul Valéry)

"Don't you find it a beautiful clean thought, a world empty of people, just uninterrupted grass, and a hare sitting up?" — D. H. Lawrence

hare sits under a baldachin of loden-green
leaves laden with kindly shades
and ghosts of a saline breeze,

hears the echo of the sea's sighing,
soughing flow, rolling over
the sands below, turning stones
birch-bark smooth,

feels light break through clouds like the loveless hearts
that clove this empty world apart,

listens to the sail-sway wind's *hush* as it moves
through cypress and yew;

remembers when the grass sang so sweet
with the psalmody of chanting birds,
the sombre matins of mourning doves.